SEATTLE CENTER

SEATTLE CENTER

Publisher GREG SAFFELL
Text by ERICA BAUERMEISTER
Contributing Photographers
CARL CLARK
CHRIS JACOBSON
VAL McCOWN
JOE POEHLMAN
MUSEUM OF HISTORY AND INDUSTRY

ISBN 0-9637816-7-7
Copyright © 2001
EMERALD POINT PRESS ®, Seattle, Washington

Printed in Hong Kong

Cover Photograph (Detail) by
CHRIS JACOBSON

SEATTLE CENTER

EMERALD POINT PRESS ®

▲

Seattle, one of the most beautiful cities in the Pacific Northwest, is located 113 miles south of the Canadian-U.S. border. Situated in the midst of an extraordinary natural setting, surrounded by two lakes and Puget Sound as well as the Olympic and Cascade mountain ranges, with the breathtaking backdrop of Mount Rainier in the distance, Seattle has long been a favorite destination of both pioneers and visitors. Perhaps known best for its precipitation, the "Emerald City" actually receives less inches of rain per year than either Washington D.C. or New York City, while the temperature reaches below freezing an average of fewer than fifteen days a year.

Voted "Best City in the West" by Money Magazine in 1998, Seattle is the home of Boeing and Microsoft, Weyerhaeuser, Amazon.com, grunge rock, and espresso coffee. The quality of life is high. Skiers can find slopes less than an hour away; water sports are as close as the nearest lake. Bike trails provide safe and

International Fountain and Space Needle After Dark About 1962

aesthetic pathways in many parts of the city. A system of ferries provides transportation to nearby islands, where growing numbers of people live year-round, commuting by water into the city. The fourteen museums, twenty-seven performing arts centers, fifty urban parks, and over 2,000 restaurants provide residents and visitors alike with entertainment, education, and enjoyment.

In the heart of all this is an area called, appropriately, the Seattle Center. Just north of downtown, near the south end of Lake Union, the seventy-four acres of the Seattle Center have become a meeting place for Seattle and the world.

The land where the Seattle Center resides has long been a gathering place. More than a hundred years ago, Northwest Native American tribes celebrated their potlatch ceremonies here. At the beginning of the 20th century, circuses and carnivals performed where the International Fountain is now. Over time, a school, auditorium, ice arena and play field were built. In the mid-1950s, the

Space Needle and Monorail Under Construction Prior to the Opening of the World's Fair in 1962.

enthusiasm generated by the idea of creating a true Civic Center for Seattle on the land turned into a bid for the 1962 World's Fair.

The theme for the World's Fair of 1962 was Science and Technology, a national preoccupation for the United States since the Russians had launched Sputnik in 1957 and the space race had begun. Thus, while the World's Fair included civic centers and theaters that would be used after the fair was over, there was a strong desire to create structures that were futuristic in both style and technology. The monorail and the Space Needle fit the bill.

The monorail, designed to carry visitors the 1.2 miles from downtown to the Seattle Center, was the first ever built in the U.S. The idea of a monorail had been around for more than a hundred years, but the aircraft technology and materials that built it had never before been used for ground transportation. Even today, the Seattle monorail is more powerful and its cars carry more passengers than any other monorail in this country.

Space Needle Under Construction With Queen Anne Hill in the Background.

If the monorail felt futuristic, the Space Needle was revolution-ary. Edward Carlson, the head of the World's Fair committee, had been traveling in Europe, and had an idea for a tall and dramatic structure similar to a television tower/elevated restaurant he had seen in Stuttgart, Germany. Jack Graham, the architect, had already started a new social phenomenon with the Northgate Mall, the first "suburban shopping center" in the U.S., and had no problem with new ideas. Through a process which included over 200 sketches and the help of many architects, the design moved from a "bal-loon" held by cables, to a saucer on a single spire, to a revolving restaurant with a planetarium dome on top and finally, to the Space Needle.

Construction was even more difficult than conceiving the de-sign. 5,850 tons of concrete went below the earth, more weight un-derground than in the tower. A special crane had to be built that could lift itself as the tower grew around it. Straight beams had to

Experience Music Project

be curved to create graceful lines. Workers swarmed up and down, working at perilous heights, sometimes in rain and snow. Perhaps the most difficult job was attaching the sun louvers on the observation deck. Workers had to slide out on the six-inch "rays" and bolt 75-pound pieces in place by hand, all the while hanging out over 515 feet of air.

But when it was finished, it was beautiful, over 600 feet, the tallest building west of the Mississippi. Its three elevators were capable of carrying 1,400 people per hour. The observation deck had 15 high-powered telescopes. The restaurant, set at 500 feet, could complete a 360 degree rotation in an hour, and was so perfectly balanced that its revolution was powered by a one-horse-power motor, less than it takes to run a vacuum cleaner. Initially painted in four colors, their names play off the technology theme: Astronaut White for the legs, Orbital Olive for the core, Re-entry Red for the halo and Galaxy Gold for the roof and underside of the top house.

Parasailing on Puget Sound

15

The Space Needle was a huge success. 2.75 million people —
more than 20,000 per day — rode its elevators during the World's
Fair, making back the costs of its construction within seven months.
In fact, the Seattle World's Fair of 1962 was one of few world's fairs
that ever made money.

The World's Fair was over on October 21, 1962, and the Seattle
Center began a new life on the next day. On October 22, the U.S.
Science Pavilion, a graceful structure which included six buildings,
five 110-foot-tall arches, and a courtyard of reflecting pools, became
the Pacific Science Center. Over 29 million people have visited since
then. With current membership of 44,000, it now has more mem-
bers than any science center in the United States. These days, ex-
hibits include a tropical butterfly house, an insect village, robotic
dinosaurs, even naked mole rats, the only cold-blooded mammals
on earth. The IMAX theater, with its huge screen and large film
format, offers a stunning visual experience. And for those who don't

Ferris Wheel at Seattle Center

19

get enough water with the Seattle rain, there is the chance to drench targets with water guns or to rotate a two-ton ball made of granite, suspended over water.

The Science Pavilion wasn't the only building that changed after the World's Fair, although eclecticism remained the name of the game. Temporary buildings were taken down, and acres of lawns and landscaping were added. The Gayway amusement area was turned into the Fun Forest, with new rides and attractions. In 1982, a new building was added with the construction of a new Seattle Repertory Theater; the Bagley Wright Theater followed in 1983. 1985 brought the Children's Museum to the lower level of the Center House. In 1991, Building 50, left over from the World's Fair, was torn down and the area turned into a sculpture garden for large and unusual works. The small, serene Peace Garden was added, the creation of the gardeners of the Seattle Center. On June 17, 2000, an 8,800 square-foot skateboard park, developed in coordination

*Experience Music Project and
Space Needle After Dark*

with the City of Seattle, King County, and the rock band Pearl Jam, was opened to the public. A $20 million renovation of the Space Needle was undertaken in 2000, adding a glass and metal nautilus-shaped two-story structure at the base with new stores and a ramp that circles the tower, barely touching it.

Perhaps one of the largest and most dramatic changes occurred most recently. On June 23, 2000, the doors of the EMP — or Experience Music Project — were opened. The museum, whose mission is to help visitors experience the innovation and creativity of popular American music, most especially of rock and roll, was the idea of former Microsoft executive Paul Allen, himself an avid fan of the late Jimi Hendrix.

A building as revolutionary as the Space Needle was when it was first built, the EMP is a creation of undulating steel and aluminum without a single right angle on its exterior. The architect, Frank O. Gehry, drew inspiration from the shapes of electric guitars which

eattle Viewed From Queen Anne

Pacific Science Cente

Washington State Ferry on Puget Sound

he bought and cut up. The bright and vivid colors come from guitars and musicians as well — blue from Fender, gold from Les Paul, purple for the Jimi Hendrix song "Purple Haze," and red for the faded red trucks that rock and roll players used to drive.

The museum features the Sky Church, a gathering hall and musical performance space with an 85-foot-tall ceiling, following Jimi Hendrix's vision of a place where people of all kinds could come together and experience music. An exhibit area features artifacts and multi-media stories from the past 100 years of music from across the country. The Artist's Journey takes visitors on an actual ride through music with the aid of lighting, audio, film, motion, and computer graphics. Those interested in creating their own music can explore in the Sound Lab using drums, keyboards, and of course, guitars. EMPlive.com takes the experience outside of the Seattle Center and into homes around the world, offering, among other things, on-line guitar lessons.

International Fountain

These days, the Seattle Center attracts over 10 million visitors a year. It is the fourth largest visitor destination site in the United States and offers over 5,000 scheduled events per year (an average of over 15 per day). Depending on when you visit, you might have the opportunity to see some of the 2,500 artists — or maybe even a public wedding — at Bumbershoot, Seattle's largest arts festival, held over Labor Day weekend. Memorial Day weekend brings the Folklife Festival, which showcases local and global culture and arts. Summer brings a chance to try out the culinary temptations of area restaurants in the Bite of Seattle, while winter offers the option of ice skating on a special rink during Winterfest. Spring brings Whirli-gig and the Seattle International Children's Festival, providing en-tertainment and education for adults and children alike.

Year-round, the Seattle Center is the home for 21 different enter-tainment, cultural, educational and sports organizations, as well as 18 restaurants. Sports fanatics come to the recently renovated Key

Experience Music Project and Monorail

Arena to watch NBA and WNBA basketball, as well as hockey. The Seattle Center's 74 acres are packed with options — the Seattle Repertory, Intiman, Bagley Wright and Seattle Children's Theaters, the Opera House and Pacific Northwest Ballet, the Flag Pavilion and Plaza, the Seattle Center House and the Memorial Stadium, Pottery Northwest and the Arts and Crafts Gallery — all create a circle around the giant International Fountain, with its sea urchin design and playful water and music. Overlooking them all, no longer the tallest building west of the Mississippi, but now one of Seattle's best-known landmarks, is the Space Needle.

Ferris Wheel and Merry-Go-Round After Dark

31

Olympus Iliad Sculpture

nnual New Year's Eve
ireworks Show

33

Flag Pavilion

Experience Music Project

Flag Pavilion and
Space Needle After Dark

Dr. Erica Bauermeister is a writer living in Seattle; she has taught at the University of Washington and Antioch University. She is co-author of *500 Great Books By Women: A Reader's Guide.*

Photography Credits

CARL CLARK
Page 21

CHRIS JACOBSON
Pages 2, 3, 15, 16, 17, 19, 25, 29, 31, 32, 34, 35, 38

VAL McCOWN
Page 33

JOE POEHLMAN
Pages 13, 23, 24, 27, 36, 37

MUSEUM OF HISTORY AND INDUSTRY
Pages 6, 9, 10